We Are All Alike

by Lola M. Schaefer

Table of Contents

How Are We All Alike?

You may think that people from different parts of the world are very different from you.

They may be different in some ways.
They may look different.
They may use different languages.

But all people are alike in some ways, too. They all **need** the same three things to live.

- All people need food.

- All people need clothes.

- All people need homes.

Why Do People Need Food?

All people need to eat food to live. Different people eat different kinds of food.

People who live in cool places often eat **fruits** like apples.

They often eat **vegetables** like beets. These are the kinds of fruits and vegetables that grow well in cool places.

People who live in warm places often eat fruits like bananas.

They often eat vegetables like peppers.

These are the kinds of fruits and vegetables that grow well in warm places.

People all around the world eat **grains**.

People who live in warm, wet places often eat rice. Rice grows well in warm, wet places.

People who live in very sunny places often eat this grain. It is like corn. It grows well in sunny places.

This grain is called **maize**.

Why Do People Need Clothes?

People need clothes to protect their bodies. Many people who live in hot places wear clothes that are long, light in color, and loose. Their clothes help them stay cool.

Loose, light-colored clothes protect people from the sun.

Many people who live in cold places wear **fur** to stay warm. Their clothes keep them safe from the cold.

Warm clothes protect people from the cold.

Many people who live in hot, wet places do not wear a lot of clothes. They need to stay cool. They let the air cool their bodies.

These people stay cool by not wearing a lot of clothes.

Why Do People Need Homes?

People need homes to stay safe. But everyone lives in different kinds of homes. Many people who live near forests have homes made from the trees around them. Their wood homes keep them safe from the wind, snow, and rain.

In some places, people build log cabins by fitting the **logs** together.

Many people who live near tall grass have homes made from the grass that is around them. Their homes protect them from the hot sun and rain.

In some places, people layer long grasses over wood frames to make grass **huts**.

Many people who live in big cities have homes in tall buildings. There is not a lot of land in big cities. People have to build homes that go up in the air.

The things we need may look different, but we all need the same things.

We are all alike!

There are many apartments in one tall building.

Glossary

fruit (FROOT): the part of a plant that has the seeds

fur (FER): the hair of an animal

grains (GRANEZ): the seeds of some plants, such as rice or corn

hut (HUT): a small house

log (LAUG): wood from a tree

maize (MAZE): corn

need (NEED): something you must have

vegetable (VEJ-tuh-bul): a plant that we eat, such as peppers or beets

Index